God's Quiet Things

God's Quiet Things

WRITTEN BY

Nancy Sweetland

ILLUSTRATED BY

Rick Stevens

William B. Eerdmans Publishing Company • Grand Rapids, Michigan

To ALL TWELVE GRANDCHILDREN
HERE TODAY AND THOSE TO COME. N.S.

To QUILLAN
AND SPECIAL THANKS TO
LORINDA AND MITCH   R.S.

© 1994 Wm. B. Eerdmans Publishing Co.
255 Jefferson Ave. S.E., Grand Rapids, Michigan 49503

Printed in Singapore

00 99 98 97 96 95 94   10 9 8 7 6 5 4 3 2 1

Library of Congress Cataloging-in-Publication Data

Sweetland, Nancy, 1934–
      God's quiet things / written by Nancy Sweetland;
  illustrated by Rick Stevens.
          p.   cm.
      Summary: Illustrations and rhyming text depict the quiet wonder
  of God's creation.
      ISBN 0-8028-5082-0
      [1. Nature — Fiction. 2. Quietude — Fiction. 3. Stories in rhyme.]
  I. Stevens, Rick, 1958–   ill. II. Title.
  PZ8.3.S9954Go   1994
  [E] — dc20
                                                    94-21229
                                                    CIP
                                                    AC

Book design by Joy Chu

Shh—
Listen.

Listen for God's quiet things,
like butterflies with velvet wings,
or raindrops making
quiet rings on water.

Listen! Can you hear a sound
from worms that wiggle underground?

Or any noise
from fish that swim
in ponds that
lilies blossom in?

Up high against
the blue, blue sky
a quiet cloud
is drifting by.

Grasses waving in the breeze
or leaves just moving in the trees —

look… and listen high and low.
God's quiet things are yours to know.

Fluffy weeds grow seeds to share

and send them sailing through the air

to gardens where the sun shines in,

where inchworms inch and spiders spin.

Do you hear
the darkness fall?
The morning dew
that comes to call?

Night comes …
Day comes …
Up so high,
the sun and moon
cross through the sky.

Look . . . and listen — everywhere.

God's quiet things are always there.

Do you hear them?

Listen.   Shhh —